# ENGLISH ABBEYS
## AND PRIORIES

JOHN CURTIS

Text by Richard Ashby

**SALMON**

# INTRODUCTION

Some Christians have always felt the need to leave the world and its temptations and practise their religion apart. Initially these people were solitaries, living alone as hermits but soon, groups of like-minded men and women came together to live in a community, to worship and work together with buildings to live in and a church in which to worship. The members of an 'order' lived according to a 'rule' which initially varied from place to place but which was later codified by St Benedict, and those who lived under his rule became known as 'Benedictines'. Many communities grew rich and powerful often employing large numbers of people. They eventually attracted the attention of Henry VIII and were suppressed, their buildings often despoiled and their assets sold to enrich the Treasury or the king's supporters. For three centuries monasticism was regarded with suspicion, but in the 19th century some orders were revived and there are now a number of communities again.

Some had their roofs and treasures removed and many ruins have little more than an arch or two surviving, but others, as at Fountains in North Yorkshire, remain almost intact. Sometimes, as at Tewkesbury or Bath, they became parish churches, while a few became cathedrals. Whatever their fate they are a reminder of the richness of English spirituality and provide a haven of tranquillity today as they have done for more than a millennium.

Tewkesbury Abbey, *Gloucestershire*

GLASTONBURY ABBEY, *Somerset*

This was the wealthiest abbey in all England after Westminster. Of Celtic origin, it grew rich on the legends of Christ's childhood visit, the Holy Grail and the graves of King Arthur and his queen Guinevere, 'discovered' by the monks in 1191. It continues to be a centre of pilgrimage today.

HEXHAM PRIORY, *Northumberland*

Most abbeys were dissolved peaceably and th inhabitants given generous pensions. Hexhar was one of the few religious houses which allied itself with the 'Pilgrimage of Grace', a people's rebellion against Henry VIII. As a result the abbot was arrested as a traitor and executed and the abbey forcibly dissolved.

**LINDISFARNE PRIORY,** *Northumberland*
This island has a very long Christian history.
In AD 634, only 40 years after Augustine
arrived in England, a community of Celtic
monks came to this windswept and isolated
place which is accessible only at low tide.
Suffering raids from the Vikings the monastery
was abandoned but re-founded in 1083.

**ST AUGUSTINE'S ABBEY,** *Kent*
Below the ruins of this Norman abbey and
its crypt in Canterbury are the remains of two
Anglo Saxon churches, one of which housed
the tomb of St Augustine. According to
legend he was sent to convert the English
by Pope Gregory, even though there was
an already thriving Celtic church here.

## BATTLE ABBEY, *Sussex*

William the Conqueror swore that, if he were successful in his invasion of England, he would found a monastery as a thanksgiving. William won the battle and four years later work started on building this great Benedictine abbey, its high altar placed on the very spot where King Harold fell. Much has been destroyed but the magnificent novices' chamber is a wonderful survivor.

## WALTHAM ABBEY, *Esse*

Augustinian canons were groups priests living together under a prior, an their life was based on a 'rule' drawn u by St Augustine. Waltham was the mo important Augustinian house in Englan and, unusually, its head was an abbo The body of King Harold was brough here for burial in the abbey church, bu the grave has long since disappeare

## CROWLAND ABBEY, *Lincolnshire*

The so-called 'Dark Ages' were punctuated by oases of civilisation. There were great Celtic monasteries, producing such treasures as the Lindisfarne Gospels and groups of hermits, usually men, who lived solitary lives of prayer and work, but who also provided spiritual counsel, assistance to travellers and the injured and often looked after roads and bridges. There was an early settlement of hermits at Crowland on an island in the Fen country. Its successor, a great Benedictine abbey, survived both fire and earthquake but like all the others it succumbed to Henry VIII. The nave became the parish church, although the roof collapsed in 1720, and now only the north aisle, with its fine stone vault, survives in use.

## MUCH WENLOCK PRIORY, *Shropshire*

Much Wenlock was originally a Saxon nunnery, founded by King Merewald of Mercia for his daughter, St Mildburg, the first abbess. In 1071 monks from Cluny, in France, established a monastery here and the saint's remains were placed in a new shrine. Parts of the church remain and three bays of the south aisle still have their vaulting. Remarkably the prior's lodging and other domestic buildings survive, having been made into a private house.

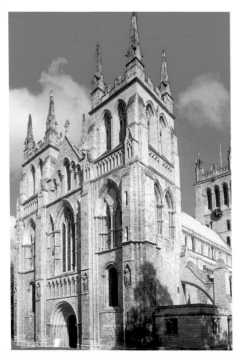

## SELBY ABBEY, *North Yorkshire*

The first monastery founded in northern England after the Conquest, Selby served both a community of Benedictine monks and the town which grew up round the abbey. It was disused for a time after the dissolution but was re-roofed and brought back into use during the reign of James I.

## GREAT MALVERN PRIORY, *Herefordshire*

Malvern Priory was founded by the monks of Westminster. It owned an important tile kiln, and some fine medieval decorated tiles and magnificent 15th century glass still decorate the interior of the church. The townsfolk purchased the great church for £20 at the dissolution after their own parish church had fallen into decay. It took the town's 100 families two years to raise the money.

## SHREWSBURY ABBEY, *Shropshire*

Once the site of the shrine of St Winifred, only the nave of the Benedictine abbey survived the dissolution and there was much restoration and rebuilding in Victorian times. Some of the domestic monastic buildings remained into the 19th century but were destroyed by the great road builder Thomas Telford when he was making the new road from London to Holyhead. A remarkable survivor from the refectory is the pulpit, from which a monk would sometimes read from the Bible or some other edifying book during meals which were otherwise taken in silence. It is separated from the abbey by the road and for a long time was surrounded by a coal yard. The novelist Ellis Peters set her 'Brother Cadfael' stories at Shrewsbury Abbey.

## CHRISTCHURCH PRIORY, *Dorset*

Christchurch was another Augustinian priory where the domestic buildings have almost all disappeared but where the great church is now the parish church for the town. It is very impressive, with much Norman work, and is the longest church in England.

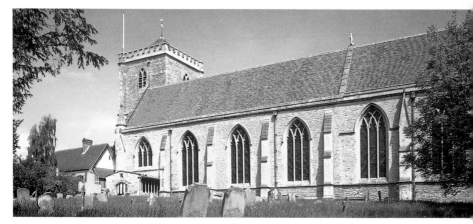

**DORCHESTER ABBEY,** *Oxfordshire*
One of the excuses for the suppression of the monasteries of England was their supposed descent into loose living and vice. At Dorchester the monks were said to spend their days in taverns, hunting or entertaining women while the abbot set a bad example with his five mistresses!

**BURY ST EDMUNDS ABBEY,** *Suffolk*
There was a major riot in Bury in 1327 when the townsfolk, who resented the power of the abbey, destroyed parts of the monastic buildings, killing several monks and capturing the abbot. Perhaps it is not surprising that after the dissolution the buildings were mostly razed to the ground.

PERSHORE ABBEY, *Worcestershire*
The citizens had been accustomed to use
the great nave of the abbey as their parish
church. At the time of the dissolution they
arranged to exchange it for the transepts and
choir and the nave and the Lady Chapel were
demolished. The north transept fell down in
1686 but the rest survives.

RIEVAULX ABBEY, *North Yorkshire*
Much of this great abbey survives, protected
by its isolation so beloved by its Cistercian
founders who were trying to regain the earlier
purity of the Benedictine 'rule' which they
believed had been corrupted. There was little
decoration in their early churches, the
architecture was plain and stark and the
monastic 'rule' was austere and hard.

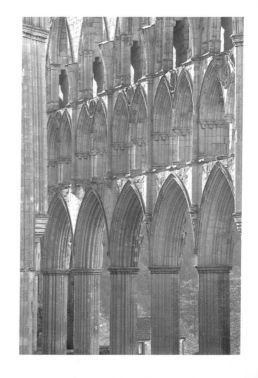

## FURNESS ABBEY, *Cumbria*

Furness Abbey, another Cistercian foundation, was situated in the remote 'Valley of Deadly Nightshade', confined by the Cumbrian hills and with its only access across the shifting sands of Morecambe Bay. Its wealth was second only to Fountains Abbey, which inevitably contributed to the relaxation of the very 'rule' it had been founded to observe.

## MALMESBURY ABBEY, *Wiltshi*

Monasteries were often great centres
learning and in them much of the ear
history of England was preserved. William
Malmesbury wrote one of the earlie
chronicles in the 12th century. Elmer, th
flying monk, launched himself off the tow
in 1005 in an attempt to fly with th
aid of wings. He survived the fa

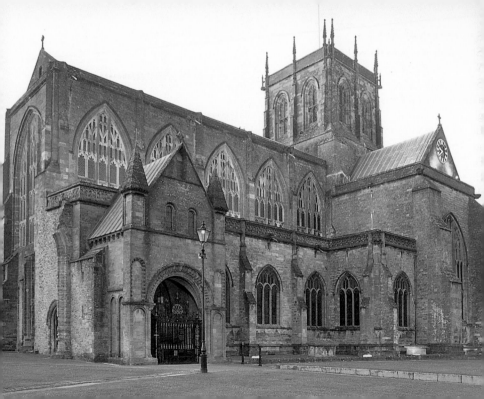

## SHERBORNE ABBEY, *Dorset*

Sherborne was once the cathedral for Wessex until it was succeeded by Old Sarum, and then by Salisbury. The abbey church reflects this former glory. Founded in 705, it became a Benedictine abbey and was rebuilt so that what remains is mostly Perpendicular architecture from the 15th century with some remains of the earlier Norman building. At the dissolution the adjoining parish church, which belonged to the town was pulled down and the abbey church itself given over to the parish. The Lady Chapel was for many years used as the house of the headmaster of the adjacent Sherborne School, but has now been restored to church use while the remaining monastic buildings have been incorporated into the school itself.

## CARTMEL PRIORY, *Cumbria*

Cartmel was a house of Augustinian canons. The monastic buildings were destroyed at the dissolution in 1537 and the roof removed from the nave, while the choir was used as the parish church. In the following century a local benefactor, George Preston of nearby Holker Hall, restored the nave and brought it back into use, fitting it with some fine Jacobean woodwork which still survives.

## BOXGROVE PRIORY, *West Sussex*

The 'opus dei', the work of God, was the
daily round of prayer and the seven 'offices'
or services which all the monks were
expected to attend unless they were ill
or away. It took place in the monastic choir
of the church. The nave was used for great
ceremonies and processions and often as the
place of worship for the parish. At Boxgrove,
though, it is the monastic choir which
survives as the people's church.

## WHITBY ABBEY, *North Yorkshire*

Whitby was the site of the famous synod
where the Celtic church submitted to that
of Rome in AD 664. The unusual double
monastery of men and women was ruled
over by the famous abbess, St Hilda, but
was destroyed in a Danish invasion and
not refounded until around 1078. The site
is spectacular, on a cliff-top above the town
and exposed to the harsh winds off the
North Sea. At the dissolution the buildings
were stripped of their timber and lead but
the shell was left as a landmark for mariners.
By the 18th century, however, it was in poor
condition and much of the west front, nave
and south transept collapsed, with the tower
following in the next century. A German
cruiser shelled the remains in World War I.

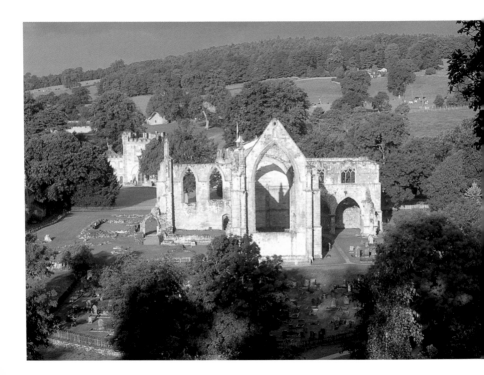

## BOLTON PRIORY, *North Yorkshire*

There were about two hundred Augustinian priories in England. They were not as large or prosperous as the great Benedictine monasteries and the rule was less austere. They often had responsibilities for the local parish and so a number of their churches survive in use. At Bolton the choir and transepts survive as romantic ruins by the River Wharfe.

## CASTLE ACRE PRIORY, *Norfolk*

Castle Acre was a Clunaic foundation and, like all others in this order, remained dependent on the mother house at Cluny in France. They had their origins in the Benedictine foundations but laid great emphasis on elaborate liturgy and ritual and their churches were highly decorated. The intricate Norman architecture at Castle Acre is superb.

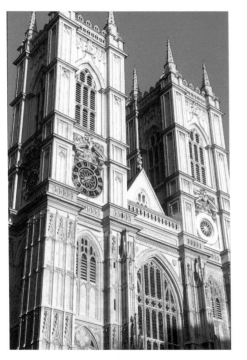

## WESTMINSTER ABBEY, *London*

Westminster began life as a Benedictine monastery, England's largest and richest, and its close connection with England's monarchy meant that it was spared the depredations which many others experienced. It was a cathedral for just ten years under Henry VIII but has ever since been a 'Royal Peculiar', under the direct control of the Monarch.

## ROMSEY ABBEY, *Hampshir*

Romsey was a nunnery. Nuns were muc fewer in number than monks and the tended to be drawn from the upper classes Often they were widows of the gentry o crusaders; sometimes they had bee separated from their husbands (there was n divorce) or had entered a nunnery when thei husbands had entered a monaster

## PRINKNASH ABBEY, *Gloucestershire*

The abbot of these Roman Catholic Benedictines dreamed of building a great church, the size of Gloucester Cathedral. Work began in 1939 but the dream could not be realised and so the new crypt became the monastic chapel with the library and the brothers' study bedrooms above. Prinknash is well known for the pottery which helps sustain the community.

## BUCKFAST ABBEY, *Devon*

The Cistercian monastery, built on the site of a Saxon abbey founded by King Canute, was destroyed at the dissolution. In 1883 the site was bought by French Benedictine monks, exiled in the religious upheavals, and they built their new church on the old foundations in an appropriate Gothic style.

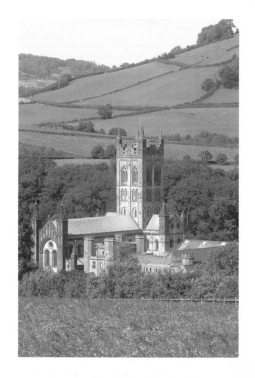

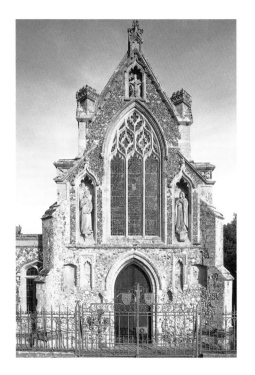

## WALSINGHAM PRIORY, *Norfolk*

Its replica of the 'Holy House', the childhood home of Jesus, made 'England's Nazareth' a great centre of pilgrimage. Henry VIII came here in 1511 but this did not save it from destruction. In the 1930s the vicar re-established a shrine in the village while the Roman Catholics adopted this 'Slipper Chapel' as their place of worship a mile away, where, in earlier times, the pilgrims left their shoes before walking barefoot to the shrine.

Published in Great Britain by J. Salmon Ltd., Sevenoaks, Kent TN13 1BB. Telephone 01732 452381.
Email enquiries@jsalmon.co.uk
Design by John Curtis. Text and photographs © John Curtis
ISBN 1-84640-032-5   Printed in Slovenia © 2006

Title page photograph: Cleeve Abbey, *Somerset*
Front cover photograph: Bath Abbey, *Somerset*
Back cover photograph: Fountains Abbey, *North Yorkshire*